Cards

A Play

Stephen Lowe

A SAMUEL FRENCH ACTING EDITION

SAMUEL FRENCH

FOUNDED 1830

SAMUELFRENCH-LONDON.CO.UK
SAMUELFRENCH.COM

CARDS

First presented at the Stephen Joseph Theatre in the Round, Scarborough, on 21st July, 1976, with the following cast of characters:

Mam	Elaine Strickland
Dad	Malcolm Hebden
Charlie	Robin Herford
Vera	Diana Bull

Directed by Alan Ayckbourn
Designed by Helga Wood

Presented at the Gate at the Latchmere, London, on 16th April, 1982, with the following cast of characters:

Mam	Janet Dale
Dad	Barry McCarthy
Charlie	Timothy Walker
Vera	Nina Edwards

The voice of the **Vicar** and **Little Boy** are heard offstage

Directed by Chris Edmund
Décor by Roger Bourke

The action of the play takes place at any east coast seaside resort

AUTHOR'S NOTE

If possible, in the foyer, there should be one or two examples of the old seaside stick-your-head-through-the-hole-and-have-a-funny-photo-taken type of boards for the audience to amuse themselves with.

CARDS

An east coast seaside resort. Winter for some, almost summer for others

The set should be minimal. Upstage, just off centre, is a flat on which is painted a seaside postcard background with a bright yellow beach, a pier, a few ships on the sea, and a bright jolly sun. Later, Routines A and B will be performed in front of this flat and various bags, containing the props, are placed nearby. There are two deckchairs downstage

The Lights come up on Big Fat Mam, who is gently gargantuan, and Wiry Old Dad (alias the Drunk), who is little but loving. They stand, looking out front, both wearing the compulsory summer seaside outfits: Mam in a red cotton dress with large white spots: Dad in shirt, braces, belt and baggy trousers. It is a very cold day and they are both freezing

Mam When do you reckin we'll be startin'? Do you know?
Dad Somebody'll tell us. They woun't leave us out here on us own — would they?

An uncertain pause

I'm thinking I should roll me trousers up.
Mam It's a bit parkie for that, duck.
Dad Best to be prepared, though. (*He rolls his trousers up*) Hankie on the head, you reckon? (*He dons his knotted hankie*)
Mam (*admiringly*) You're a real pro, you are.
Dad Man should take a bit of pride in what he does. (*He pauses*)
Mam Bit chilly out here. You sure you're all right?
Dad Bracing. (*He shivers*)
Mam (*quietly*) Me feet are killing me.
Dad Have a sit down in a bit, duck. Take the weight off 'em on them deckchairs. When they've finished with us, might even have a bit of a paddle. Depends what they've got in mind for us.
Mam I don't fancy that much, luv.
Dad Salt water. Best thing out for feet. (*Kindly*) Soon be home, luv.

Mam Coun't we sit down now?
Dad Best to wait, luv. Show willing.
Mam (*stoically*) 'Spect you're right.

Long pause for shivers

Dad (*looking off*) There's the vicar.

They both smile off

Mam Morning, Vicar.
Dad How do!

The voice of the Vicar—who is pungently pithy—is heard off

Vicar's voice I'm pissed off wi' all this pissin' about.
Mam (*politely*) Always the same, innit?

They resume their former statuesque manner. Pause

Dad (*sighing*) I should have gone into Church.
Mam (*sadly*) I know.
Dad But it won't to be.
Mam You'd have been lovely in the pulpit. You've got the class for
  it. I've always said that. You're wasted here.
Dad Too late now.
Mam You could still be a Methodist.
Dad Not the same thing.
Mam Not enough class.
Dad Don't get me wrong, I'm not calling them. I think they're
  probably fine in their own way, but it in't the same thing as C. of
  E. Different all together. Difficult to explain.
Mam These things always are. Will they be much longer?
Dad Would you like to put me coat round you?
Mam (*giggling*) Hardly fit, would it, duck?
Dad (*laughing, and the first time really looking at her*) You could
  always wear it as a scarf!

They both laugh, but it dies down and the cold returns

Mam (*quietly*) Oh ay, you'd look lovely in black.

They are both lost in thought.

Dad (*eventually*) I hope we don't have too many pisspot jokes this
  year. They used to be harmless, but they seem to have got nastier
  as time goes on. I'll be exposing meself soon.

Mam (*horrified*) Lord, no, duck!
Dad It won't be long now.
Mam Oh, no. Would you like a corn beef?
Dad No, luv, ta, better wait.
Mam Have we missed aught?
Dad Better check. Get your list.

Mam checks through the list of props and ticks them off as Dad produces objects from the various bags and places them in position for Routine A

Right.
Mam Bucket and spade.
Dad Ay.
Mam Ice-cream cornets.
Dad Ay.
Mam Stethoscope.
Dad Ay.
Mam Whiskey.
Dad Ay.
Mam Little stick of Blackpool rock.
Dad Little stick of Blackpool rock. Do you remember that?
Mam Go on. Give us a bit.

Dad sings the first few lines of the chorus of "Little Stick of Blackpool Rock" and plays the rock like a ukelele

Blackpool pier. Nineteen forty-six. George Formby. Oh, that were lovely.
Dad Cleaning Windows?

Mam cheers up and starts to speak the first part of the chorus from "Leaning on the Lampost", she and Dad alternate the lines

Dad Oh, me—
Mam Oh, my.
Dad A real pro.
Mam Bags of talent.
Dad Dead now.

A nostalgic pause. Mam blows her nose. Dad goes back to the bags

Red nose.
Mam Ay.

Dad Hair net.
Mam Ay.
Dad Beer mug.
Mam Ay.
Dad Rolling pin.
Mam Ay.
Dad Jerry.
Mam Ay.
Dad That's the lot.
Mam (*looking at the list*) Braces.
Dad Braces. (*He searches for them, then realizes he's wearing them*)
    Braces!
Mam (*absently*) I wonder what's holding them up?
Dad (*confused*) Pardon?
Mam I s'pose they might be doing the Scotsman's bit. Takes a bit
    of time to get the wind blowing in the right direction.
Dad Ay, I s'pose it must.
Mam Let's sit down.
Dad Hang on another couple of minutes. I think they'd like to
    catch us out. You know what it's like now — all this super
    efficiency, and technique and — darling this and darling that. It
    in't like it used to be when old Don was around.
Mam Don who?
Dad Donald. You remember Donald, duck.
Mam (*disbelievingly*) Donald Duck?
Dad No, not Donald Duck, Donald what's his name. Scottish
    name. Donald Mc— Mc— it's on the tip of me — Gill. Donald
    McGill!
Mam Oh ay. Donald McGill, duck. I remember him. A lovely
    bloke. Real comic he was.
Dad Fine drawer, as well, he was. Little bit of art, them cards were.
Mam Told our Vera, people used to pin 'em up next to "Bless This
    Home".
Dad Did 'n' all.
Mam Our best years wi' Don.
Dad Dead now.

Long pause

Mam Me feet are killin' me.
Dad (*melancholic*) I've not given you what I'd hoped to give you.

Mam You've always done your best.

Dad I dreamt of better. I din't intend we should end up here.

Mam Force of circumstances, luv. Never really had a chance. Coun't have expected angels to do better. (*She touches his face gently*)

Dad (*deeply moved, turning away*) Where's our Charlie gone and got to?

Mam He's probably practising his leer.

Dad Do you remember mine. (*He leers*)

Mam Could I forget? Beautiful to behold it was.

Dad They say me dad had a good 'un. Me mam said I took after him in that.

Mam He must have been summat then.

Dad (*smiling*) Are you trying to butter me up?

Mam (*seriously*) I've never regretted it.

Dad (*sniffing, turning away*) Our Vera's not around either.

Mam She'll be putting the padding in. It's a bit tricky that.

Dad You never needed much. I were right proud of you.

Mam I s'pose I was a bit of a natural, really.

Dad You carried it well.

Mam Well, I had a lot to carry.

Dad And it's still lovely stuff.

Mam Don't see much of it nowadays, do we? I wish, now and again, they might let me wear summat more flattering. It's all right in this job, till you're about twenty-one. They encourage you to wear aught, lovely long-legged type of stuff, and then, when you've done the bride bit, naught on at all, really, you wake up and you're down for Mam-in-law, the fat old bag, forty-five and fiery.

Dad Well, that's the job, luv.

Mam I know, but why in't there naught between? Whatever happened to the in-between years? (*She pauses*) I'm going to take me shoes off.

Dad (*looking at the audience*) Hang on, luv. I think they're coming!

Mam It's no good. They're killing me. (*She bends over to untie them, revealing the inevitable, giant, red-knickered bum*)

Dad They've caught you!

ROUTINE A

The Postcard

NB. In this sequence, the characters take tableaux derived from traditional seaside postcards, and the caption is heard via the front-of-house speakers. It should be played very fast with the Lights snapping on for each pose and then a Black-out after the caption has been read. Music can be used. The two lists of jokes given in Routine A and Routine B (which follows later) are simply suggestions, worked out by the author and the members of the first production. Because of the technical problems involved and, also, to familiarize the artists with the world of seaside postcards, it seemed inadvisable to fix these routines. The following list, then, is something to which one can add, subtract, or ignore

1 **Mam** (*still bending over as she was before*) My cheeks are getting rosy since we came here!

2 **Dad** (*still in the same pose as before*) There's a lovely sandy bottom here. You ought to see it!

3 **Mam** } (*together; swimming bottoms up*)
   Dad   } Of the bottomless sea, the poets sing,
             } But down here we've quite a different thing.

4 **Mam** (*to skeleton sitting between them*) What's the food like at your hotel?

5 **Dad** (*with a telescope, leaning dangerously out of a window*) I can see the sea from my bedroom window!

6 **Dad** (*as Doctor to Mam in bed*) All you want, you know, is a little sun and air.
   Mam Oh, Doctor! You naughty man! At my time of life?

7 **Dad** (*cuddling Mam*) Holding you brings out the animal in me.
   Mam Never mind. I'm not frightened of mice!

8 **Mam** I'm just going to look under the bed and see if there's a marauder there.
   Dad (*holding up a chamber pot*) It's all right, luv. It's on this side.

9 **Mam** (*in bed, wearing the chamber pot*) Oh, look, luv. They've given me one of those boudoir hats!
Dad You silly a'peth. You've got the bow at the back!

10 **Mam** (*looking in a mirror*) I was only a slip of a thing when I met you!
Dad Yes, you've certainly slipped a bit since then!

11 **Mam** I never knew you were so stupid when I married you!
Dad You must have known I was a bit daft when I proposed.

12 **Mam** (*looking over Dad's shoulder as he reads a girlie magazine*) What's she got that I haven't got more of?

13 **Mam** I'm just going to weigh myself.
Dad What's the poor thing done to you?

14 **Vicar's voice** You surely will admit the existence of a supreme and unchangeable will?
Dad Not half. I married it!

15 **Mam** (*with a rolling pin*) Drink is your enemy!
Dad (*with a whiskey bottle*) Thou shalt love thy enemy!

16 **Mam** The police said you drank nineteen pints and then pinched a gentleman's bowler hat.
Dad After nineteen pints I needed something!

17 **Dad** (*lying flat out by a parking meter*) Put a shilling in. I'm parked for the night.

18 **Dad** (*holding up a loo seat*) I thought it was just the thing for your mam's picture.

19 **Mam** (*to the Audience*) My old man has suffered from constriction ever since he was demoralized from the army.

Music ends the routine. The Lights come up as before but Mam and Dad still hold the positions. Pause

Dad I think they've gone, luv.
Mam Thank God! It's probably their lunch break. They keep to themselves, don't they? I suppose they get bored with it, not really their cup of tea. They always look so cold in those Afghan coats, poor devils. Can we sit down now?
Dad I think we could now.

*They come forward and sit on the deckchairs. Mam starts unpacking
lunch*

Mam Corn beef?
Dad Have you got egg?
Mam I was in such a rush this morning ...
Dad Corn beef'll be lovely. I don't know that I don't prefer corn
  beef. Egg's just habit, really. It always seems to be egg whenever
  we do this.
Mam It makes a change.

They eat

Dad Did you think it were different from last year?
Mam There was summat a bit funny about 'em. Coun't quite put
  me finger on it——
Dad Well, we got spared most of the urinal jokes.
Mam Mind you, they were always more the Scotsman and the
  vicar's bit than ours. (*After reflection*) And the little boy did a fair
  amount of wee-wee stuff.
Dad Do you know, I haven't seen him this year.
Mam (*in between mouthfuls*) I've got a funny feeling that that
  second lecherous young man is him.
Dad What makes you think that?
Mam Well, he keeps smiling at me in a funny way.
Dad Good Lord! He's sprouted up a bit then!
Mam Our Charlie had better watch out with his leer, or he'll soon
  be out on his ear.
Dad (*looking as though something is bothering him — perhaps that
  last rhyme?*) Things are certainly changing fast.
Mam Ay.
Dad Did you bring the flask?
Mam Course. Just a mo. (*She ferrets it out*)
Dad I should have gone into the Church. Made a good home for
  us.
Mam I know.
Dad Where's the spirit in a po?
Mam (*remembering*) Eh, we didn't do that one?
Dad Which one?
Mam You know, that one with you, one hand on a bottle of
  whiskey, t'other on a bright blue piss pot, with your red nose

shining and the caption: "Here we are full to the brim with high spirits in sunny Skegness."

She laughs but Dad is not affected

Dad I worry about this, you know. Years ago, when we were getting going as lecherous and buxom and then as honeymoon couple, just the same as our Charlie and Vera now, and Mam and Dad before us, well, then I thought it were a bit of fun, couple of bob out of it, nothing crude.

Mam It were a laugh. No harm in it.

Dad Took the edge off them windy war days out at Cleethorpes or Whitby or whatever.

Mam A private joke to keep our spirits up.

Dad Now it's big business. They bring their poodles wi' 'em, all wrapped up, and leave 'em locked up in the cars so they don't get sand in their nose. And who, out of the old bunch, made out of it? We're still here, playing the old uns——

Mam And our kids doing the same as our folks before us——

Dad 'Cept cruder——

Mam And look on us, and seeing what we got out of it ...

Dad Naught.

She fills his cup for him

Mam (*after hesitating*) Dad, they asked our Vera if she'd do the hole-in-the-bottom-of-the-bath-tub gag, but instead of the old way, with her back to us, they wanted her to be—exposed out front.

Dad I've been expecting that. What did she say?

Mam She didn't say.

Pause. They begin to nod off

Do you think you might still get into Church?

Dad Bit late in the day now.

Mam I s'pose so.

Dad It's a lovely bit of sea round here. You don't very often get a chance to really appreciate it, what with all the rushing about. It makes it all worthwhile.

Mam Corn beef, luv?

Dad I think I'll just have a little think.

The Lights fade as they settle themselves in

Charlie and Vera enter upstage. He is Leering Young Man (and Bridegroom) and is rather ratty. She is Buxom Young Beauty (and Bride) — a Macclesfield Monroe

ROUTINE B

As before, Charlie and Vera adopt poses while the caption is heard via the front-of-house speakers, with a Black-out after each caption has been read. Routine B is slightly more "risqué" than Mam and Dad's, and even faster. The story line of the pictures here, with the elements of courtship and marriage, is stronger than in A so beware any considerable deviations in improvised work. The implications are probably more important than the laughs. Music starts and the Lights come up on Charlie and Vera in the first pose before the flat

1 **Charlie** (*as Doctor*) Big breaths now.
   Vera Yeth, and I'm only thixteen!

2 **Charlie** (*to shop assistant*) Do you keep stationery, miss?
   Vera Well, I wriggle about a bit sometimes.

3 **Vera** (*bending down to select an article*) Can I show you anything further, sir?

4 **Charlie** If I told you you had a smashing figure would you hold it against me?

5 **Charlie** (*embracing Vera*) Would you call for help if I made love to you?
   Vera Only if you needed it.

6 **Charlie** (*as Policeman*) I'd like to go for a swim but I don't want to get me truncheon wet.

7 **Charlie** (*as Policeman*) Now, miss, can you identify the man who exposed himself?
   Vera I'm afraid I can't. I didn't look at his face!

8 **Vera** (*coming out of the woods with Charlie*) Father was right — you don't have to drink and smoke to have a good time.

9 **Vera** (*to Charlie*) I promised Mam I'd be good — was I?

10 **Charlie** (*to the Audience*) She's a nice girl. Doesn't smoke or drink and swears only when it slips out.

11 Charlie (*as Doctor*) Have you ever been X-rayed?
Vera No, but I've been ultra-violated a couple of times.

12 Charlie (*as Doctor*) Do you ever get a tickle in the morning, miss?
Vera I used to, Doctor, but I changed me milkman.

13 Charlie (*as Doctor*) I've got some good news for you, Mrs Ramsbottom.
Vera Miss Ramsbottom.
Charlie Then I've got some bad news for you.

14 Vera (*holding a baby*) I was only going to let him kiss me, but he said that gave you germs.

15 *Vera and Charlie as bride and groom*
Little Boy's voice Dad says it's a shotgun wedding. Can I see the gun, mister?

The Honeymoon

16 Charlie (*to Vera who wears a short nightdress*) You haven't been down the corridor in that, have you?
Vera Don't worry. I pulled it over my head so no-one could see me.

17 Charlie Your nightdress is looking a bit the worse for wear, isn't it?
Vera Well, it's seen lots of ups and downs in its time.

18 Vera (*looking down the blankets*) Oh! Have we used it all up in one night?

19 Vera (*on the phone, as husband lies exhausted on the floor*) I think the honeymoon is over, Mum.

A Black-out ends the routine. Two spots come up on Charlie and Vera as they dress at opposite sides of the stage. Charlie has bright blue trousers

Vera (*eventually*) 'Bout what you said, Charlie.
Charlie (*combing his hair back*) Yes, Vera, my little pigeon.
Vera Set me thinking, Charlie. Do you think when we're Mam and Dad's age, we'll end up like them? You know, trousers rolled up, hankie on the head, and all the time you wanting to be a vicar.

Charlie (*chuckling*) The Church's never really been up my street,
Vera.

Vera No, but you know, what you were saying, Charlie. Failed,
Charlie. In a rut, Charlie. A nameless couple of old pros on
postcards. I'm not blaming 'em, you know, but somehow I think
they could have done summat a bit better for themselves. Become
a cartoon in the *Reveille*, for instance.

Charlie (*distastefully*) The *Reveille*? I'm not one to call your family,
Vera, but well, they're a bit lacking in drive, like, and that's where
the big difference lies.

Vera I'm not quite with you, Charlie.

Charlie (*picking a hair off his bright blue trousers*) I've got drive.

Vera (*pleased*) Oh. (*Then, after more sober thought*) Where you
going to drive me to, Charlie?

Charlie crosses to his "Ginger Rogers"; the two spots merge

Charlie I'm going to drive us to the top, Vera. Me and you, we're
moving right on out of these cheap postcards, and moving right
on into cartoons, and we're not stopping there, Vera, oh no,
we're going to go much higher than that—me and you, Vera,
together, we're going to become a syndicated strip.

Vera (*ecstatically*) A syndicated strip!

Charlie Nothing less.

Vera Wow!

*They go back to their dressing. Vera, in her undies, begins a strip
routine*

(*After a pause, uneasily*) Charlie, does a syndicated strip mean I
have to take my clothes off to a regular beat?

Charlie It's nothing to do with you taking your clothes off. Well,
not directly. It's what I was talking about with them. A daily
cartoon series that's shown in dozens of papers all over the
world, like Dagwood and Blondie, and The Gambols, and
Barbarella, and Modesty Blaise, and Jane and Daughter of Jane,
and things.

Vera Andy Capp!

Charlie Well, yes. Andy Capp is a sort of syndicated strip, but it's
not quite what I had in mind for us. It's a trifle *passé*.

Vera I've never had one of those.

Charlie It's a bit common. To be blunt, it's more your Mam and

Dad's cup of tea, 'cept there's too many like them trying to break into the market. No, there's going to be summat a bit classier for us.

They are now dressed and start to pack up their props. The Lights begin to come up slowly so that there is a daylight effect by the time they go to see Mam and Dad

Vera You mean, I won't have to come out here in the middle of winter, and take me clothes off?

Charlie No more seasonal work for us, constantly being laid off. Soon we'll be up there with Mr and Mrs Gambol, and Mr and Mrs Blondie, in a nice semi with central heating, little car, funny little dog to bring me slippers, whist drives round the block in winter, couple of bright, funny little kids. We'll be doin' very nicely for oursen.

Vera It sounds lovely. When do we move in?

Charlie Well, not straight away, like, it takes a bit of time, but they've promised they'll see us all right. You know, you can't just dive into that sort of thing. You've got to learn to crawl, before you can fly, or you're likely to get drowned. Got to get acclimatized first.

Vera I'm not quite with you, Charlie.

Charlie Well, it's very simple. It's like what they were saying — we've been living in this very narrow little world in Biggleswade. Bigotted Biggleswade as that man in the leather hot pants called it, and we've got to get more with it first.

Vera (*persisting*) With what?

Charlie (*perturbed*) Well, it's a matter of, well, for example, we've just been doing this rather coarse stuff, which is all right for your mam and dad, it being catered for their taste, but it's out of touch with what's happening now. People are freer now than they used to be, and they want more adult stuff — intelligent, sophisticated.

Vera (*with surprising insight*) Oh, you mean doing that nudist camp joke with your trilby hanging on your——

Charlie (*unwillingly*) Well, that sort of thing but——

Vera And me fully exposed sort of thing.

Charlie Full frontal it's called, Vera, and what's the harm? (*Winningly*) You've got a beautiful body, my love.

Vera Me mam won't like it.

Charlie (*taking her hand*) It's only for a bit, darling, until we get a bit more sophisticated, then we get the little house and dog and car and kids and all, and with the syndicate, we'll be out of all this for good.

Vera Well, if you think it's right.

Charlie Course it is. Better than staying here.

Vera They promised you, did they?

Charlie Better than in writing.

Vera Better tell me mam, then.

Charlie (*as neither of them have made a move*) It's only right for people with our talent. We shou'nt be stuck here, year after year. It in't right.

Vera Well . . .

Charlie Do we have to tell them right now?

Vera I think it's only right.

Charlie They don't want us to end up the same way as they have. Am I right?

Vera You're right.

Charlie Right then.

Vera Right away.

Charlie Right.

Charlie puts his best foot forward, and arrives there behind Vera. Mam and Dad are apparently asleep

Vera Are you awake, Mam?

Mam Course I am, luv. I was just watching the light on the water. Don't disturb your dad, though. He likes his little think. Hello, Charlie, have you done your bit?

Charlie For the time being.

Mam I don't know if they're finished with us yet. I'd like to go home. In't it lovely out here? If it won't so cold it'd be beautiful. You all right, Charlie?

Charlie I'm all right.

Mam Not much of a joke being on comic postcards, is it? Few hours hard work, then months of hanging about.

Charlie That's what we've been talking about.

Mam I was just remembering the first time I clapped eyes on you, Charlie. I doubt you'd remember it being so long ago.

Charlie I don't remember.

Mam Your mam, second tart as she was then, brought you. You'd be about two or three, and a lovely little lad you were as well. I remember the first postcard you and Vera ever did. You were looking down Vera's pants, and she was looking down yours and you were saying, "It must have fell off when you ran for the bus," and I knew then you were fated for each other. And sure enough, you grew into a fine lecherous young man, and Vera into a lovely buxom young girl, and now you're the honeymoon couple. Ay.

Charlie (*who may have heard it before*) That's all very interesting, but——

Mam That's how me and your dad started, Vera.

Charlie I think you had mentioned it, Mam.

Mam He was saying something a bit different. I can't remember what it was. I was too young mesen then.

Charlie Well, that sort of relates to what we wanted to—— ·

Dad suddenly jumps up, with a certain wild air about him

Dad Have you seen Jock, the Scot?

Vera I think he's down with the thistles, Dad.

Dad stalks to the back of the stage to check

Dad No, he must have nipped off for a nip. I've missed him.

Vera What did you want him for, Dad?

Dad Well, it all come over me, sudden.

Mam What did, duck?

Dad Our Jock and his memoirs.

Charlie Memoirs? What could happen to a Scotsman for him to write memoirs about?

Dad Jock's writing about serving on postcards during war. You'd be too young to remember that but me and your mam were honeymoon couple in those days, and Jock asked me if I remembered aught about those times that was sort of patriotic—— the Dunkirk spirit, and as I was lying here, meditating, it all come back to me . . .

Mam Must have been the corn beef.

Dad In them days, cards used to matter more than they do now. Soldiers used to carry 'em about in their pockets, summat of home. Anyway, this particular incident concerned me mam and dad, your grans, with him being a little air-raid warden trying to push your gran into an air-raid shelter, and her jammed solid. Now your gran, Vera, you'd hardly remember, but, well, your mam's a big lass, but your gran took the biscuit. Not to put too fine a point on it, your gran had a bum the size of a zepplin. I'll never forget it. There she was, one giant, red-white-and-blue-knickered bum, jammed in this door, and dear old dad pushing for all he's worth, and the caption read, that our dad was saying——

Mam "It's not the GERMAN bombs I'm frightened of!"

Mam and Dad go into tucks of laughter. Vera laughs, Charlie smiles sympathetically

Dad Well, I s'pose you have to see it really. It's a visual thing. But it were funny.
Mam Funny how they come back to you.
Dad It is that.

Charlie coughs

Mam Dad, I think the kids have got summat to say to us.
Dad What's on your chest, then, lad?
Charlie Well, me and Vera were thinking——
Dad In that case, lad, you'd better sit down!
Charlie Er——
Mam Now then, Dad!
Dad Ay. Sorry. Just a little joke, that's all. Go on, lad.
Charlie Well, we were thinking that it was time that we got out of all this and got into summat better, if you see what I mean.
Dad (*pleased*) I do. I do, indeed, lad. In the state the industry's in at the moment I wouldn't advise you to stay on. There's naught here for a man to take pride in any more, and as far as I can see, it's only going to get worse. I hoped you'd come to such a decision, lad. What sort of thing did you have in mind as doing?
Vera We're going to work in syn——er . . .
Charlie Syndicated strips.
Dad (*impressed*) Syndicated strips, eh? Well, now that really is big time. Own little house, car, funny dog an' all. Well, in't that a nice surprise, and here we were worrying about you without cause.
Mam (*getting up and kissing them both*) Oh, that's lovely. Lovely news.
Dad What sort of material will you be working in, then, Charlie? Not the gangster or Garth-type stuff, I shoun't think?
Charlie Well, that sort of detail's not quite fixed, yet. It takes a bit of time to find the exact format what's best for you.

Dad Oh, I can appreciate that but I s'pose it'll be mainly the domestic family type of thing, won't it?

Charlie I should think so, yes. Er—Mam——

Dad (*more insistently*) You should think so? You mean, you should know so. You've seen the contract, haven't you?

Charlie Not exactly.

Dad Well, what vaguely have you seen?

Charlie Well, they han't had time to draw up contract yet.

Dad I'd have thought you'd have learned by now that nothing is settled in this business until it's drawn up, signed and stamped. I don't know what your family taught you.

Mam Now then, Dad, don't spoil it for them.

Dad Spoil it? Spoil what? I'd like to know what I'm accused of spoiling. He comes here and says they're all set to go into syndicated strips, and then he says they don't know what sort, and they haven't got a paper nor nothing drawn up, and you say, don't spoil it. Spoil what? If you ask me, they're doing note but romancing.

Vera No, we're not, Dad. Honest. It's just that we have to become a bit more sophisticated before we——

Charlie What Vera is trying to say is that there's an initial training period before we can picture what our final position will be, so to speak.

Dad Oh, a training period. I see now. Well, that's reasonable. Course, it'll be a new world for you. You'll have to practise a bit. That's only proper. Well, I'm sorry for losing me temper with you. I was just worried about the disappointment you might be letting yourself in for. But a training period, well, that's only reasonable, innit?

Mam Course it is, luv. Now, why don't we settle down and have a nice corn beef?

Dad Good idea.

Mam and Dad re-seat themselves. The kids sit on the ground. Mam offers round the corn beef

Mam Vera?

Vera Oh, thanks, Mam.

Charlie (*quietly*) Vera.

Vera Yes, Charlie.

Charlie You're watching your figure, Vera.

Vera Yes, Charlie. (*She puts it back*)
Mam Charlie?
Charlie No, thank you, Mother. I've just had me liver pâté.
Mam I didn't know you'd been ill, Charlie.
Dad Corn beef won't harm your liver, lad.
Mam I should have brought egg. Egg's ever so light on your stomach. Are you sure?
Charlie No, thank you.
Mam Dad?
Dad Lovely.

Mam and Dad munch merrily away. Mam pours tea

What sort of training have you to do then?
Vera We have to do more sophisticated things.
Charlie What Vera means is——
Dad What do you mean, Vera?
Vera Well, I don't——
Charlie The sort of thing they want us to develop is——
Dad Now then, Charlie. I was asking our Vera. What sort of thing, Vera?
Vera (*frightened*) Sophisticated things.
Mam Don't badger her, Dad.
Dad I'm just asking a civil question. Go on, Vera.
Vera Things—more for the time now.
Dad How do you mean?
Vera With-it things.
Dad (*suspicious*) Charlie, where are you going for this training?
Charlie Well, initially, at first, for the time being, we haven't got to go far, in fact, we haven't got to go anywhere, to start with. But we move up later.
Dad Let me get this straight. For the time being, you're to stay here, doing with-it things as training to be sophisticated?
Charlie Well, roughly.
Dad But they've never had syndicated strips round here, so what'll you be working on?
Charlie Well, for the moment, we'll still be on postcards, just temporary.
Dad You'll be doing with-it things on postcards?
Charlie Well, up to a point—yes.
Dad (*quietly*) I see. Do you see, Mam?

Mam Yes.

A long, shocked silence. Vera and Charlie are trying to pretend they're somewhere, anywhere, else

Dad (*eventually exploding out of his deckchair*) Dirty postcards. Our daughter's going to do dirty postcards. Filth. What do you say to that, Mother?
Mam (*quietly*) I'm too taken aback to say aught, luv.
Dad (*angrily*) Well, I'm not. I haven't worked all my life beside the sea to see my daughter up to her eyes in muck. I say no! NO! You'll not do it.
Vera Dad——
Dad You heard me. I'm not one for laying down the law, but, by God, this time I'll have to. You'll not do it. You hear me?
Vera Yes, Dad.
Charlie Dad.
Dad And as for you, Charlie, I've always treated you like me own. But you've bitterly hurt me, lad. There has to be some standards. I know we're fighting a losing battle on these postcards, but that don't mean you have to float with whatever filthy currents happen to be in sway. Sometimes you have to stand firm. That's what standards are laid down for, for people to stand by them. And not be bought off. I can't allow it, lad.
Charlie (*angrily*) You can't stop it, Mr Ramsbottom. You can't stop it.
Dad Yer what?
Charlie Vera's my wife now. It's not just a case of the leering young man and buxom lass. I asked for her hand and you gave her away, and we became the honeymoon couple. She's mine now. You can't force her what to do.

Dad looks as though he's going to burst a blood vessel. He makes to attack Charlie but is restrained by Mam

You've made your bed and you can lie in it, but we're getting out, and you're not going to stop us.
Vera (*moving to Dad*) Dad, don't——
Charlie Come here, Vera!

She crosses back

Dad You swine!

Charlie I'm not taking your daughter to a fate worse than death, Mr Ramsbottom. Everybody's doing it now.

Mam Calm yourself, Dad. There's note we can do.

Dad (*with considerable control*) You can let me go now. (*With dignity*) I can't persuade you the error of your ways?

Charlie Never!

Dad Then I must take final steps to put an end to it. (*In a highly dignified manner, he turns and starts walking away*)

Mam No, Dad. NO! Don't do it.

Dad Do what, woman?

Mam It's not worth it. Think of me left behind without you. How will I manage?

Dad What you going on about? I'm not going to drown meself. Not when I hold all the cards.

Charlie (*nervously*) What do you mean?

Dad Ah! Got you worried now an't I? You din't think a Ramsbottom would give in that easily, did you?

Vera What you going to do, Dad?

Dad I'll tell you what I'm not going to do. I'm not going to stand back and have the only daughter of mine parading herself without a parallel in front of the eyes of "sophisticated" people, that's what I'm not going to do.

Mam Yes, but what are you going to do?

Dad (*proudly*) I'll tell you. I'm going to see our masters, and put it to them straight. If they use my daughter on these dirty postcards, Mam and Dad are going to quit. It's as simple as that.

Charlie Oh no!

Dad (*crossing to under Charlie's nose*) Got you worried, eh? And rightly, 'cos you know that they're not going to throw away a lifetime of tradition and experience for the likes of someone like you they can pick up on any street corner in Chelsea.

Charlie (*genuinely concerned*) No, don't do that, Mr Ramsbottom.

Dad I don't like doing it, lad, but I've got my standards and I can't act different. (*Gently*) I'm sorry. But just admit you're beat, and we'll forget the whole sordid affair, eh?

Charlie I can't do that.

Dad Right, lad. I'm sorry an' all that, honest I am, but you've left me no choice. (*He turns to go*)

Charlie They've sacked you!

A stunned silence

Dad Wha'?
Charlie (*upset*) They're retiring you. They asked me to break it to
  you.
Dad You're lying.
Charlie I've got a letter. (*He takes a letter from his jacket pocket*)
Mam Oh, Dad.
Dad But they can't retire us. Nobody else could do it.
Charlie Said they were bringing in somebody else — somebody
  more willing.
Vera I didn't know, Dad.
Dad Why din't they tell me?
Charlie Thought I could break it better.
Dad Ay.

*Mam crosses, takes the letter very gently from Charlie, and carries it
across to Dad. He opens it and reads it*

  A month's pay. Me dad got a gold watch. And a party. Do you
  remember that booze-up we had?
Mam Ay.
Dad He drank a pint of guinness out of me mam's slipper, and did a
  little boy routine with her knickers pulled up round his neck.
  (*After a pause*) That were a booze-up, that were.
Mam (*crying silently*) Ay.
Charlie I din't want to break it like this.
Vera Oh Dad, I am sorry.
Dad Course not, lad. You coun't help it.
Charlie But me and Vera, we've got our own lives to lead.
Dad Naught to be said, really.
Charlie Well, we'd best be off and put in some work. We've had a
  long lunch break.
Dad Best not to keep them hanging on.
Charlie Right. Well, we'll see you later then.
Mam Course. Though we'll probably have gone home before
  teatime.
Charlie Well, we'll pop by and have a drink tonight.
Vera I'm ever so sorry, Dad.
Charlie We'll be off then.
Mam Right.
Charlie Right-o.
Dad (*nodding*) Right.

Charlie and Vera exit

Let's sit down, shall we, luv?

They both sit down. Mam is crying

Mam Would you like another corn beef? I made too many.
Dad Why are you crying, luv?
Mam You know who's going to be the next Mam and Dad, don't
   you?
Dad Yes.
Mam I couldn't tell them.
Dad Neither could I.

Pause. Very distantly, very softly, seaside organ music is heard

I should have gone in Church.
Mam Circumstances wouldn't allow.

The Lights fade slowly to Black-out

FURNITURE AND PROPERTY LIST

On stage: 2 deckchairs downstage. *By them:* **Mam**'s bag containing corn beef sandwiches, flask of tea, cups, prop list, pen, handkerchief

Bags. *In them:* bucket and spade, ice-cream cornets, stethoscope, bottle of whiskey, stick of rock, comic red nose, hair net, beer mug, rolling pin, chamber pot

Dad's jacket

FOR ROUTINE A

Skeleton **(Mam)**
Telescope **(Dad)**
Chamber pot **(Dad)**
Chamber pot **(Mam)**
Mirror **(Mam)**
Girlie magazine **(Dad)**
Rolling pin **(Mam)**
Whiskey bottle **(Dad)**
Parking meter **(Dad)**
Loo seat **(Dad)**

FOR ROUTINE B

Stethoscope **(Charlie)**
Police helmet **(Charlie)**
Baby **(Vera)**
Blankets **(Vera)**
Telephone **(Vera)**

Personal: **Dad:** knotted handkerchief
Charlie: comb, letter in jacket pocket

LIGHTING PLOT

Property fittings required: nil
Exterior. The same throughout

To open: General daylight effect

Cue 1	**Dad:** "They've caught you!" *Change to spots on* **Mam** *and* **Dad**	(Page 5)
	ROUTINE A *Please refer to pages 6 and 7*	
Cue 2	After final Black-out in Routine A *Bring up general daylight effect*	(Page 7)
Cue 3	**Dad:** ". . . just have a little think." *Fade to Black-out*	(Page 9)
	ROUTINE B *Please refer to pages 10 and 11*	
Cue 4	After final Black-out in Routine B *Bring up two follow spots on* **Charlie** *and* **Vera**	(Page 11)
Cue 5	**Charlie** and **Vera** pack up their props *Slowly bring up general daylight effect*	(Page 13)
Cue 6	**Mam:** "Circumstances wouldn't allow." *Slow fade to Black-out*	(Page 22)

EFFECTS PLOT

Cue 1   **Dad:** "Neither could I." (*Pause*)   (Page 22)
         Very distant, soft, seaside organ music

9 780573 120299